A Nut Pie for Jud

Written by Emily Beth Gerard

This is Jud's tree.

This is the bud on Jud's tree.

This is the nut from the bud on Jud's tree.

This is Jud's nut pie made from the nut
on Jud's tree.

Jud cut the nut pie.

But Mom said no.

This is Jud's pie.

A Nut Pie for Jud

Written by Emily Beth Gerard

Modern Curriculum Press
An Imprint of Pearson Learning
299 Jefferson Road, P.O. Box 480
Parsippany, NJ 07054-0480
http://www.mcschool.com
1-800-321-3106

Design and production by Bill SMITH STUDIO

All photographs are by Pearson Learning unless otherwise noted. Aristock, Inc./Roger Idenden 2, 4. © Joyce Photographics/Photo Researchers, Inc. 3.

ISBN: 0-8136-1972-6 Modern Curriculum Press

7 8 9 10 SP 01 00 99

The Bus

Written by Joaquim Alvarez

Illustrated by Lynn Munsinger

SCHOLASTIC INC.

New York   Toronto   London   Auckland   Sydney
Mexico City   New Delhi   Hong Kong   Buenos Aires

The sun is up.
Gus is up.

Russ is up.
Russ sees the bus.
It is up the hill!

3

Gus runs up.
Gus huffs and puffs.

Russ runs up.

But where is the bus?

Russ sees it.
Russ runs down.
Gus runs down.

6

Gus and Russ hit mud!

Gus and Russ hit the tub.

Text copyright © 2003 by Scholastic Inc.
Illustrations copyright © 2003 by Lynn Munsinger.
All rights reserved. Published by Scholastic Inc.
Printed in the U.S.A.

ISBN 0-439-53338-4

SCHOLASTIC, SCHOLASTIC READINGLINE, and associated logos and designs are trademarks and/or registered trademarks of Scholastic Inc.

3 4 5 6 7 8 9 10   23   12 11 10 09 08 07 06 05 04

SCHOLASTIC
ReadingLine™

This edition is only
available for distribution
through the school market.